Love Me Slender

Poems About Love

Sophie Hannah

Duffy & Snellgrove

Sydney

Published by Duffy & Snellgrove in 2000
PO Box 177 Potts Point NSW 1335 Australia
info@duffyandsnellgrove.com.au

Poems first published in Britain by Carcanet Press in
The Hero and the Girl Next Door (1995) *Hotels Like Houses* (1996)
and *Leaving and Leaving You* (1999)

Cover Design by Alex Snellgrove
Cover Illustration by Rosanna Vecchio
Photograph of Sophie Hannah (back cover) by Peter Collie
Typeset by Gail MacCallum

ISBN 1 875989 69 2

visit our website: www.duffyandsnellgrove.com.au

Sophie Hannah is 29 years old and lives
in Yorkshire, England. Her witty and
heart-breaking poems have been widely acclaimed
in Britain, where her three books have
found a remarkably big audience.

The Poetry Review has declared:
'Shall I put it in capitals?
SOPHIE HANNAH IS A GENIUS.'

SOFT COMPANION

He sat in the under-heated flat, alone,
Usefully passing time (he thought by choice),
Not missing anything, until the phone
Brought him the soft companion of your voice,

And then he looked around himself and saw
The scraps of clothing on the floor, in shreds,
And felt his keys hang heavy in the door.
He thought of powdered milk and single beds.

Unsure of him, you said, 'It's only me,'
Meaning not quite enough, but you were right:
Yours was the only face he hoped to see
And only you remembered him tonight.

SYMPTOMS

Although you have given me a stomach upset,
weak knees, a lurching heart, a fuzzy brain,
a high-pitched laugh, a monumental phone bill,
a feeling of unworthiness, sharp pain
when you are somewhere else, a guilty conscience,
a longing, and a dread of what's in store,
a pulse rate for the *Guinness Book of Records* –
life now is better than it was before.

Although you have given me a raging temper,
insomnia, a rising sense of panic,
a hopeless challenge, bouts of introspection,
raw, bitten nails, a voice that's strangely manic,
a selfish streak, a fear of isolation,
a silly smile, lips that are chapped and sore,
a running joke, a risk, an inspiration –
life now is better than it was before.

Although you have given me a premonition,
chattering teeth, a goal, a lot to lose,
a granted wish, mixed motives, superstitions,
hang-ups and headaches, fear of awful news,
a bubble in my throat, a dare to swallow,
a crack of light under a closing door,
the crude, fantastic prospect of forever –
life now is better than it was before.

The Affair

The lamp post bends his head. His face is red
above the frozen fringes of the street.
Dishevelled night is climbing into bed.
She strokes the waking clock, then steals the sheet.

Something disturbs the symmetry of hedges;
a recent scandal seeping through the grass.
The breathing curtains lose their heavy edges,
touched by the light that settles on the glass.

A small dog kicks the pavement into stretching.
The postbox mouth hangs open for receiving.
I almost hear a taxi driver fetching
your suitcase. Very soon you will be leaving.

FIVE SONNETS

When I am Famous

When I am famous, in the years to come,
I know how keen you'll be to share the glory;
When journalists whip out a hefty sum
Before your nose, to make you sell our story,
You'll have no qualms. I, therefore, will expect
Full details of our sex life in *The Sun*.
I will not sue you, nor will I object
In any way – I'll treat it as good fun.
Make sure to give them all the dirty bits.
The truth gets dull – why not throw in some lies,
Some strange inventions? Say I've got three tits
Or four. Meanwhile, I've got a nice surprise
In store for you – I'll make you tremble yet:
I know about your flower-pressing set.

Wrong Again

I did the right thing once (may God reward me);
Restrained myself. I took a moral stance.
Virtue, I found, was not my thing – it bored me
Rigid, and I would like another chance
To earn myself a wicked reputation
Equal to yours. I'll match you sin for sin.
Lies, promiscuity, inebriation –
It all sounds lovely. When can we begin?
I used to be afraid of rumours spreading.
You made my fear seem fussy, immature.
Here's my new motto, then: just change the bedding
And carry on exactly as before.
A single, happy night beneath your quilt
Is all I want. I'll risk post-coital guilt.

The Philanderer's Ansaphone Message

I'm not at home to take your call. Bad luck,
But leave your number and I'll be in touch.
You'll hear from me next time I want a fuck,
(My love, my darling). Thank you very much.
Please leave your name – I'll add it to my list,
That way I won't forget. One does lose track...
But I can guarantee that when I'm pissed
I shall be keen to get you in the sack.
I knew this ansaphone would come in handy –
Voice after female voice I've got recorded.
I play the tape back when I'm feeling randy
And one by one my ladies are rewarded.
My system works supremely well, I've found.
Wait by the phone until your turn comes round.

One-Track Mind

Why does she take unnecessary trips?
She lives just opposite a row of shops.
She went to Crewe to buy a bag of chips.
She went to Birmingham to buy lamb chops.

She has no time for aeroplanes or boats.
She cannot get enough of British Rail.
She went to Liverpool for Quaker Oats
Then Halifax to buy the *Daily Mail*.

She went to Chester for a pair of tights.
Every weekend she's up and down some track.
She went to York for twenty Marlboro Lights.
She went to Stalybridge and came straight back.

Once, on her way to Hull for cottage cheese,
She saw him. All he said was *Tickets, please*.

A Fairly Universal Set

Whoever cleans your windows once a week,
Whoever stuffs your letters through the door,
Whoever you'd get in to fix a leak –
I resent all of these and plenty more.

Men on the bus and women in the street,
Religious nuts who ring your bell at dawn,
Any chiropodist who's touched your feet,
Canvassers, tramps, whoever mows your lawn,

Your colleagues, friends, acquaintances (both sexes),
People with whom you've shared a cigarette,
Your enemies, and, most of all, your exes,
Everyone you have ever seen or met,

Voices you might from time to time have heard,
The speaking clock. Jealous is not the word.

Before Sherratt & Hughes Became Waterstone's

Romantic entanglements often occur
In a pub or a railway station,
But being a writer I tend to prefer
A suitably bookish location.

I've never liked nightclubs, nor am I the sort
To go for a snog in the loos.
By far the most interesting place to cavort
Is the ground floor of Sherratt & Hughes.

I've seen a few customers looking dismayed,
Too British to voice their objection,
But how can I help it? I like to get laid
Just in front of the poetry section.

Most people prefer a luxurious setting –
A Mediterranean cruise,
But to my mind, the place most conducive to petting
Is the ground floor of Sherratt & Hughes.

All it takes is one glimpse of a gold-lettered spine
On those lovingly organised shelves
And a human encounter seems almost divine –
Not just sex, but a merging of selves.

I have never been someone who strictly adheres
To what's proper – I do as I choose.
(I go down very well with the male cashiers
On the ground floor of Sherratt & Hughes.)

THE GIFT

I am saving my money
to buy you a raw potato.

I will scrub it with my nailbrush
and bathe it in my basin.

I will cut out your initials
from its smooth, brown jacket.

I will gift-wrap it in pink paper
and tie it with pink ribbons.

I will place it in a shoe-box
on a bed of tissue paper.

I will deliver it to your doorstep,
wearing pink shoes.

You will stare at it crossly at first,
as if it were a baby.

You will take it inside quickly
to stop the neighbours staring.

You will not know where to put it.
You will be afraid to hold it.

You will hide it in your bedroom
to protect it from stray glances.

It will live in the furthest corner
forever, and embarrass you.

MINDING HIS BOOTS

He likes to walk around barefoot
while I mind his boots – the only part
of him which can stand still.

Pieces of broken glass and stones
don't seem to cut; his soles are tough,
dark like leather, skin socks.

Here is the trail of flat-crushed daisies
his going left behind, small white
and yellow crumbs in grass.

He is unreachable, framed
in an accidental afternoon
that lingers, hungry for souvenirs.

These boots which he leaves in my care
will belong to me longer than he will belong
to any earth, any air.

A DAY TOO LATE

You meet a man. You're looking for a hero,
Which you pretend he is. A day too late
You realise his sex appeal is zero
And you begin to dread the second date.

You'd love to stand him up but he's too clever –
He knows by heart your work and home address.
Last night he said he'd stay with you forever.
You fear he might have meant it. What a mess!

That's when you start regretting his existence.
It's all his fault. You hate him with a passion.
You hate his love, his kindness, his persistence.
He's too intense. His clothes are out of fashion.

Shortly you reach the stage of desperation.
At first you thought about behaving well
And giving him an honest explanation.
Now all you want to say is 'Go to Hell',

And even that seems just a touch too gentle.
Deep down, the thing that makes you want to weep
Is knowing that you once felt sentimental
About this wholly unattractive creep.

SECOND HELPING OF YOUR HEART

1

I can't remember saying that I wanted this,
But these things happen. (Enter other platitudes.)
I was your midnight scrap. You left your haunted kiss
On my cold lips, without once changing attitudes.

A woman packs a suitcase in the south.
Calf-muscles ache. She may be feeling old tonight,
Or be in bed. Her understudy's mouth
Treats dirty fag-ends like small bars of gold tonight.

I can't remember mixing the ingredients.
Did I or did I not play any part in this?
(Enter a childhood training in obedience.)
Is there a second helping of your heart in this?

The inefficiency of most removal men
Is something that you cannot bear to think about.
Why I should bother chasing your approval when
I disapprove is something I must drink about.

Here, under chilly light and wooden beams,
My thumbnail is too long. It's like a talon.
Here is your parting gift: disruptive dreams
From four till seven. (Enter Woody Allen.)

2

If we examine ratios of power, praise
Becomes a farce. I start to doubt its origin
And its sincerity. Your leaning tower ways
Make bowls of women, fit for slopping porridge in.

Do I have any choice but to give way to you,
Here, in this echo-box? The shadows creep outside.
The sober cynic in me wants to say to you,
'Why bother with me, dear, when there are sheep outside?'

But you're too genuine, too off-the-cuff to be
Kept at a distance, treated with disparagement.
Let us not mention what you're old enough to be
Or that you're still not quite sure what your marriage meant.

So. Do you really think my work is saleable?
And will your confidence in me deflate a bit
If I declare my body unavailable,
All heavy, disbelieving five foot eight of it?

(Enter a fear of alcohol-dependency,
Tomorrow morning, what the hell I'll say to you.)
I can't risk heights and depths. I have a tendency
To step around such things. And so good day to you.

TRAINERS ALL TURN GREY
(AFTER ROBERT FROST'S
'NOTHING GOLD CAN STAY')

You buy your trainers new.
They cost a bob or two.
At first they're clean and white,
The laces thick and tight.
Then they must touch the ground –
(You have to walk around).
You learn to your dismay
Trainers all turn grey.

FOR THE FOLLOWING REASONS

Because strands of wool do not trail
from the sleeves of my jumper.

Because I would never stop reading a book
three pages before the end.

Because I brush teeth not tooth.

Because I wait for the aeroplane
to land before stepping outside.

Because I like to do things properly.

Because I like people to know what I mean
and do not stop talking or writing until they do.

Because I don't waste time on jigsaws
with only one piece,

or send letters without my signature,

or eat lunch without digesting it,

or brush all the hair to the left of my head,
ignoring what grows on the right.

Because I can only tolerate moments
if they are firmly lodged in hours.

Because I am orderly and extrapolate
neat patterns from the most uncertain things

you will be hearing from me again.

Two Rondels

The End of Love

The end of love should be a big event.
It should involve the hiring of a hall.
Why the hell not? It happens to us all.
Why should it pass without acknowledgement?

Suits should be dry-cleaned, invitations sent.
Whatever form it takes – a tiff, a brawl –
The end of love should be a big event.
It should involve the hiring of a hall.

Better than the unquestioning descent
Into the trap of silence, than the crawl
From visible to hidden, door to wall.

Get the announcements made, the money spent.
The end of love should be a big event.
It should involve the hiring of a hall.

More Trouble Than Fun

We cannot undo what we've done
But we don't have to do any more.
What on earth are we doing it for
If it's so much more trouble than fun?

If you want, I can act like a nun.
I'll be meek and incredibly pure.
We cannot undo what we've done
But we don't have to do any more.

Just remember that you were the one
Who complained that your life was a bore.
Now you suddenly feel insecure.

Will it help if you panic and run?
We cannot undo what we've done
But we don't have to do any more.

Amusing Myself

Here is the form I should have signed,
The book I should be reading.
Every attempt is undermined
By thoughts of you, stampeding.
I try to still them; am resigned
To not succeeding.

Here is the card I would have sent,
The fruit I would be peeling
If every second wasn't spent
On you, but while each feeling
Goes where its predecessor went
There'll be no healing.

Here are the words I'm scared to use.
You wouldn't catch me saying
This to your face, though I amuse
Myself and God by praying
That you'll be back; next time confuse
Me more by staying.

THE ANSWER

Why do you give the impression that you'd rather
not be loved? You almost tell people not to bother.
Why are you neither one thing nor the other?

Why do you fluctuate between ticks and crosses,
alternate between flippancy and neurosis?
Won't you confirm or contradict my guesses?

What is it that you do, by simply sitting
with your elbows raised, that makes me sick of waiting?
Why is your absence tantamount to cheating?

I know you're real, which means you must pay taxes,
catch colds and snore. I know you know what sex is.
Still, there is something in you that never mixes,

something that smells like the air in silver boxes.

It makes me suddenly afraid of asking,
suddenly sure of all the things I'm risking.

FRIENDS AGAIN

Let's sort this out. Make no more cherry
scones for the man that stole my jewels
and I'll stop spitting in your sherry.
Both of us have been fools.

Here, you can have my rope and pins
if you give up your hooks and nails
and we'll agree to wear wide grins
for subsequent betrayals.

Even a bond as firm as this
friendship cannot withstand attacks
if they are too direct; let's hiss
behind each other's backs.

In future, when I tread thick soil
into your house, I'll hide my feet,
and if you have to be disloyal
please try to be discreet.

Two Love Poems

Poem for a Valentine Card

You won't find any hints
Enclosed, no cryptic clues, no fingerprints,

Nothing about the gender,
Background or occupation of the sender.

Anonymous, unseen –
You're dealing with the all-time king or queen

Of undercover loves.
The author of this valentine wore gloves.

Red Mist

You could wear different shoes,
Lose all the worthwhile things you have to lose;

You could go mad and howl
From a high tree through darkness, like an owl –

No part of me would change
However sick you were, however strange.

Your future, near and distant,
Is safe, as long as I remain consistent.

If, one day, you commit
A crime, I'll burn all evidence of it.

When it arrives, my doom
Will be a red mist entering the room.

Miracles Start like This

Unlikely though it is
That you remember, let alone adore me,
Miracles start like this –
God, or yourself, or Jim
May fix it for me.

It's the impossibility
That makes recovered sight miraculous
And the same mystery
That unblinds eyes
Could do some work for us.

Perhaps a need like mine
For you would be considered too small-scale
To attract much divine
Concern, in which case
This appeal may fail.

I've heard of people walking into flames
And coming out unhurt. Though I hold tight to
Faith, I would like some names
As well, of lesser saviours
I could write to.

YOUR STREET AGAIN

'Guess who I saw last night?' was all she said.
That, and the answer (you), was all it took,
And now I'm leafing through my A-Z
To find your street again. I had to look

Four years ago, and memorise the way:
Palatine, Central, Burton – halfway there.
I don't intend to visit you today
As I did then, and so I shouldn't care

Which road comes after which and where they lead.
I do, though. I repeat them name by name.
My house is here and yours is there. I need
To prove the space between them stays the same.

THE TROUBLE WITH KEEPING IN TOUCH

In case you've ever asked yourself how long
A girl can sit and chew a ball-point pen,
Put down some words and then decide they're wrong
And cross the whole lot out and start again;

In case you've wondered how the record stands,
Take it from me (I know because I hold it) –
It's infinite; it constantly expands.
The truth can change just when you think you've told it.

Whatever may have happened to us both
Since I last smiled and waved and said goodnight to you,
Our lives continue growing, and the growth
Makes it impossible for me to write to you.

GHAZAL

Imagine that a man who never writes
Walks on the planet Mars in cricket whites

Looking for signs of life which isn't there.
He walks through hot red days and dark red nights

Across a surface which is rough and bare.
He feels confused; he's come to see the sights

But there are none, and nobody to share
His empty mouth, his sudden fear of heights.

Nine of his cigarettes are going spare.
The tenth is for himself, and that he lights.

Something's familiar now. He starts to swear.
He stumbles through bizarre, one-sided fights.

Meanwhile you're stuck on Earth without the fare.
In any case, there are no scheduled flights.

And all the love you send is lost in air,
And all your words stick in the sky like kites.

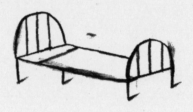

LOVE ME SLENDER

'Lovely Lesley lost six stone and won her man'
(headline from the *Sun*, 30 June 1993)

You have to be size ten to get a bloke.
You must be slim, petite, and never podgy.
Since Stout is out you're left with Diet Coke
And other things that taste extremely dodgy.

You must be thin. Don't make me say it twice.
Size ten, or even twelve, but never fatter.
You may, in other ways, be very nice
But if you're overweight it doesn't matter.

You have to shed the pounds. It's such a drag.
You can't rely on brains or sense of humour.
It isn't true that many men will shag
Virtually anyone – that's just a rumour.

You need a model's figure, skin and bone,
Straight up and down without a single curve,
Unless you want to end up on your own,
Which, frankly, would be just what you deserve.

The Hero and the Girl Next Door

This story has at least one side.
The source is quite reliable.
The hero did his best. He tried,
But it was not a viable
Prospect, and so he burned his boats,
He cut his losses, changed his mind,
Dry-cleaned his most attractive coats
And left the girl next door behind.

His Christmas list had shed a name.
The girl next door had shed some tears,
But she was utterly to blame,
Had been, in fact, for several years.
Rewind. The lady vanishes.
Press stop, fast forward, then eject.
And what a silly girl she is.
And does she honestly expect...

So this is provocation, then,
And this is what they call just cause
And this is how you see it when
The hero is a friend of yours.
Another soldier saves his skin.
Another wrinkle ironed out.
You bet. You roll the dice. You win.
There is no reasonable doubt.

Absence Makes the Heart Grow Henry

Ann was the love of Colin's life
Until the day he went to meet her.
Later she became his wife
But absence makes the heart grow Peter.

Jack was obsessed with Debbie's writing.
Then one day he caught the train
And found the woman less exciting.
Absence makes the heart grow Jane.

I love you when you're not around.
If we come face to face again we
Stand to lose by being found,
For absence makes the heart grow Henry.

THE ONLY POINT IS DECIMAL

Ninety per cent of places are not worth going.
Ninety per cent of jobs are not worth doing.
Ninety per cent of men are not worth knowing.
Ninety per cent of women are not worth screwing.

> An attitude like yours must take some practice.
> Part apathetic, mostly condescending,
> Lukewarm then spiky, vichyssoise-cum-cactus,
> That's you, my friend. Or are you just pretending?

Ninety per cent of books are not worth reading.
Ninety per cent of songs are not worth singing.
Ninety per cent of advice is not worth heeding.
Ninety per cent of numbers are not worth ringing.

> Life passes by, but you are not impressed.
> You'd rather be a lonely couch potato
> Than compromise. There's no point getting dressed
> For anyone less erudite than Plato.

Ninety per cent of chances are not worth taking.
Ninety per cent of corners are not worth turning.
Ninety per cent of hands are not worth shaking.
Ninety per cent of candles are not worth burning.

> And all that I can think is what a shame.
> What are the odds you'll wonder where I went?
> The chances of you knowing why I came?
> Point zero zero zero one per cent.

THE KEYBOARD AND THE MOUSE

I am myself and in my house
But if I had my way
I'd be the keyboard and the mouse
Under your hands all day.

I'd be the C prompt on the screen.
We could have had some fun
This morning, if I'd only been
Word Perfect 5.1.

I'd be your hard and floppy discs,
I'd be your laser jet,
Your ampersands and asterisks –
I'd be in Somerset

Rotating on your swivel chair.
The journey takes a while
But press return and I'll be there.
Do not delete this file.

ALTERING THE ANGLE

Quick, summon up your out-of-bed persona;
Start acting like you met me at a conference
Ages ago. Throw in a bit of indifference.
This month's adventure stars the cowboy loner,
And, look, it's almost time to do something spontaneous.

For all your talk of changes and the future
You wouldn't dream of altering the angle
Of your ponytail, relinquishing the single
Newspaper life. Under that cloak of culture
Your past consumes your present like a vulture.

I'm flexible, but why should I adapt
To being systematically ignored
By somebody whose scores don't make the board?
And as for warmth you might as well be wrapped
In clingfilm on an isolation ward.

Proud of how unemotional you are,
You coast along – never a peak or trough –
And I'm your novelty inside a jar;
You count the seconds of my wearing off,
Talk about how you'd like to travel far
Away from me. I hope the sea is rough.

So, what's the next meticulously planned
Escapade going to be? Will you expand
Your consciousness, experiment with lust,
Make a few notes and think you've got it sussed,
The science of excitement in your hand?

Well, here's goodbye. Experiment with that.
You're far too big a space for me to fill,
And even with the greatest strength of will
I can't hallucinate a rolling hill
On land that is predominantly flat.

HOTELS LIKE HOUSES

She is the one who takes a shine
to ceilings and to floors,
whose eye finds room for every line
scratched on the wardrobe doors.

She thinks in terms of thick red rope
around the bed, a plaque
above the hardened bathroom soap.
He's always first to pack.

If their affair has awkward spells,
what's bound to cause the rows is
that he treats houses like hotels
and she, hotels like houses.

Two Sonnets

Darling Sweatheart

He couldn't spell. The letters were addressed
to *Darling Sweatheart*, though he acted mean
when I was with him. Probably the best
present he gave me was some margarine –

a tub of Stork, half full. It wasn't wrapped.
He shrugged and said *You might as well have this.*
He'd find excuses, say his lips were chapped
in an attempt to dodge my weekly kiss.

He'd made a comprehensive wedding plan
involving just the two of us. No way
were guests allowed. His dog would be Best Man.
I dithered. *What a life* he used to say,

Let's have a kid. If we get skint, we'll sell it.
He wasn't bad. It's just the way I tell it.

Credit for the Card

She took the credit for the card I sent.
It's bad enough that you are hers, not mine.
How dare she, after all the time I spent
Choosing and writing out your Valentine,
Pretend it came from her, after the date
And its significance had slipped her mind?
She saw her chance before it was too late
And claimed my card – mysterious, unsigned –
Became the face behind my question mark.
Now there's too much at stake. She can't confess.
She has conspired to keep you in the dark
Which fact, she knows, would make you like her less.
Her lips are sealed. She lied and she forgot
Valentine's Day. I didn't. Mine are not.

FAIR TO SAY

It's fair to say you own a boat. It's yours.
Nothing luxurious. A rowing boat.
First it springs holes and then you lose the oars.
It's when the thing can barely stay afloat
Let alone speed you off to foreign shores –
At that point you no longer have a boat.

You rent a flat, a corrugated box,
No fancy furnishings, no welcome mat.
One day the landlord changes all the locks.
A dog moves in. It tries to kill your cat.
It's when the door stays closed, despite your knocks –
At that point you no longer have a flat.

You've got a boss. You've worked for him for years.
He is a firm, authoritative boss
Until one day the office disappears.
You ask him what to do. He's at a loss.
He looks away and covers up his ears –
At that point you no longer have a boss.

As for your man, the things he used to do
Like smile and speak, watch movies, make a plan,
Listen to music, kiss – to name a few –
He's given up, as if some kind of ban
Were on them all. When somebody who blew
Hot now blows cold and you've done all you can –
At that point you no longer have a man.

When his turned back makes one bed feel like two –
At that point you no longer have a clue.

LUSTING AFTER WALTER KNIFE

They mention him without intent
And you pretend you haven't heard
Anything more than what was meant
Because his name's a household word.

Imagine – loving Peter Chair
Would make deciding where to sit
Almost impossible to bear
If you connected him with it,

Or lusting after Walter Knife –
One move to spread your margarine
Might make you want to stab his wife;
Not what things are but what they mean

To you, so dig a hole and hide
Unless his name is Pete or Loam
And if the man's called Mountainside
You might be better off at home.

The Pros and the Cons

He'll be pleased if I phone to ask him how he is.
It will make me look considerate and he likes considerate people.

He'll be reassured to see that I haven't lost interest,
which might make him happy and then I'll have done him a favour.

If I phone him right now I'll get to speak to him sooner
than I will if I sit around waiting for him to phone me.

He might not want to phone me from work in case someone hears him
and begins (or continues) to suspect that there's something between us.

If I want to and don't, aren't I being a bit immature?
We're both adults. Does it matter, with adults, who makes the first move?

But there's always the chance he'll back off if I come on too strong.
The less keen I appear, the more keen he's likely to be,

and I phoned him twice on Thursday and once on Friday.
He must therefore be fully aware that it's his turn, not mine.

If I make it too easy for him he'll assume I'm too easy,
while if I make no effort, that leaves him with more of a challenge.

I should demonstrate that I have a sense of proportion.
His work must come first for a while and I shouldn't mind waiting.

For all I know he could have gone off me already
and if I don't phone I can always say, later, that I went off him first.

INTO HIS PLANS

The truth, which on my more possessive days
Lurks in the background, spoiling all the fun,
That I am not the only game he plays,
Neither am I the most important one,
I've always known. I knew before I fell
Into his plans. I knew because he said,
And, flattered that he wanted me as well,
I didn't wish he wanted me instead
At that stage. Now I'm feeling discontent
And longing for a more familiar mess –
Having been many people's main event,
People who've hurt me more and liked me less
Than he does – also knowing that it's wrong
To think this way, not thinking it for long.

PERSON SPECIFICATION

The ideal candidate for the position
of soulmate to the all-important you
should say she loves you, of her own volition
every five minutes, and it should be true.

She must be motivated and ambitious
but feminine. She will be good at art,
at homely things. Her meals should be nutritious.
The ideal candidate will win your heart

with her prowess in bed. She will look stunning
in public, turn at least ten heads per day.
She should do most of (if not all) the running
and be prepared for marriage straight away.

Points will be lost for boring occupations,
excessive mood swings, drugs and other men.
To those who fail, your deep commiserations.
This post will not be advertised again.

TWO POEMS ABOUT MUSIC

Her Kind of Music

Her kind of music was a song
About a broken heart,
While his was complicated, long,
And labelled 'modern art'

With links to the chromatic scale.
The opera he wrote,
To her ears, was a lengthy wail
Upon a single note.

She struggled to acquire his taste
(As frequently occurs),
While, with enthusiastic haste,
He did away with hers.

When a Poet Loves a Composer

One look at him and I forgot,
Embarrassingly soon,
That music ought to have, if not
Lyrics, at least a tune.

He's highbrow in a big, big way
But when he sees that I'm
The one, he'll think that it's okay
For poetry to rhyme.

The Mind I Lose

Whether the things I feel are true
or just illusion on my part,
I think that I'm in love with you
and wouldn't want to doubt my heart.

You say my heart may not exist.
I know it does, but isn't what
I once believed. This adds a twist,
the like of which can save a plot.

Feelings and thoughts are kept apart
unfairly by the words we choose.
Find me a better name than heart
by which to call the mind I lose.

SOFT-HANDED MAN

She couldn't love a man who had soft hands
and didn't do constructive things with wood,
but if she met one that she loved, she could.
She's right to say we all make strange demands
and right to think that no one understands.
Hard hands are not indicative of good

character, don't infallibly belong
to rugged, silent types who rarely shave,
who are, in equal measures, kind and brave.
Just over the horizon there's a strong
soft-handed man waiting to prove her wrong,
and when a person proves you wrong, they save

acres of mind you were about to close
and turn it into habitable land.
Each time you hold an unexpected hand
and stare at features that you never chose,
you're dealing with authority that knows
better than you how well things can be planned.

LOSS ADJUSTER

Scale down your expectations once again
from rest of life to years to one whole night
to will he wander past a phone or pen.
If he would only either ring or write.
Get real and scale those expectations down
from conversation to a single word —
seen through the window of a shop in town
if not by you then by a trusted third
party, or, if a sighting is too much
to hope for (as undoubtedly it is)
scale down your hopes and aim to see or touch
someone whose name sounds similar to his.
A scale of one to ten. Two weeks ago
he dared to keep you waiting while he slept.
Scale down much further and today's poor show
tomorrow you'll be happy to accept.

NOD AND SMILE

'You couldn't take him anywhere,' she said,
'Even your best friends wouldn't want to know.'
She must have thought I harboured in my head
A glossy guide to places we could go.

'There's nowhere I could take him,' I agree.
She takes the opportunity to breathe a
Sigh of relief, then she turns back to me
And says, 'He'd never let you leave him either.'

'I couldn't ever leave him,' I concede.
There's much agreement in our brief exchange.
She's thrilled and I am not, but we're agreed
That circumstances won't improve or change,

That I could save myself a lot of pain.
There's not a word she says I don't believe –
Much easier only to entertain
Thoughts of a person you can take, or leave.

THE GOOD LOSER

I have portrayed temptation as amusing.
Now he can either waver or abstain.
His is a superior kind of losing
And mine is an inferior brand of gain.

His sacrifice, his self-imposed restriction
Will get through this controversy intact
For his is a superior kind of fiction
And mine is an inferior brand of fact.

I have displayed my most attractive feature
And he his least, yet still the match seems odd.
For I am a superior kind of creature
And he is an inferior brand of god

And if he cuts me off without a warning
His is the book from which I'll take a leaf
For his is a superior kind of mourning
And ours a most inferior brand of grief.

Occupational Hazard

He has slept with accountants and brokers,
With a cowgirl (well, someone from Healds).
He has slept with non-smokers and smokers
In commercial and cultural fields.

He has slept with book-keepers, book-binders,
Slept with auditors, florists, PAs,
Child psychologists, even child minders,
With directors of firms and of plays.

He has slept with the stupid and clever.
He has slept with the rich and the poor
But he sadly admits that he's never
Slept with a poet before.

Real poets are rare, he confesses,
While it's easy to find a cashier.
So I give him some poets' addresses
And consider a change of career.

AGAINST ROAD-BUILDING

He hated roads. He loved the land.
He tended to forget
Or else he didn't understand
That roads were how we met.

He loved long walks. He hated cars.
He often put them down.
Without them, though, I'd have reached Mars
Before I reached his town.

Now that I've seen bad air pervade
An atmosphere once sweet
I wish the car was never made
That drove me to his street.

Now that I've felt a world explode
As I had not before
I wish they'd never built the road
That led me to his door.

RONDEAU REDOUBLÉ

He likes the soup but doesn't like the spoon.
We hold opposing views on means and ends.
It's funny now, but it would matter soon
If we shared more than chinese food and friends.

In case he breaks the only time he bends,
He drinks the coffee, leaves the macaroon.
He says, as though pure anarchy descends,
He likes the soup but doesn't like the spoon.

I've sat in restaurants all afternoon,
Fallen for all the culinary trends
But to admit this seems inopportune.
We hold opposing views on means and ends.

Normally I am someone who defends
High living, but I let him call the tune
During these strange, occasional weekends.
It's funny now, but it would matter soon;

The earth won't sprout a ladder to the moon
Though we make compromises and amends.
It would be like December next to June
If we shared more than chinese food and friends.

Sometimes we clash, sometimes our difference blends
And the cold air turns hot in the balloon.
I tell myself (in case success depends
On attitude) that though he hates the spoon,
He likes the soup.

FOUR SONNETS

Unsavoury (Could Almost Pass for Sweet)

He parks where he is not allowed to park
and does what he is ill-advised to do.
As reassuring as a question mark,
his words are neither sensible nor true
but still I let him know that he's preferred.
His nod confirms that he can be discreet.
The way he twists the meaning of a word
unsavoury could almost pass for sweet.

Sweet: in my weaker moments, everyone
rallies around and soon I have a list
of twenty reasons why I ought to run.
My reason is the only one they've missed:
not all the bad things he may do or be
but that he's better at them all than me.

Never His

I freeze as I'm about to write his name.
Politely, he reminds me who he is.
What can I say that won't sound trite or lame –
I could forget some names, but never his?
So I say nothing, simply write it down,
hand him the envelope and let him leave,
though I'm inclined to chase him all round town
to put this right, tamper with clocks, retrieve
the eyes that wavered and the hand that shook,
the hesitation he perceived as tact,
the blush he understandably mistook
for loss of memory (which now, in fact,
is sharper than it was, and will replay
him telling me his name all night, all day).

Typecasting

Not knowing you, I thought I knew your type –
how you'd behave, the sort of thing you'd say.
I guessed you'd be inclined to take a swipe
at anybody getting in your way.
I told my friends you were like this, like that,
had you evading taxes, cutting throats,
gave you a line in patronising chat,
presented my imaginings as quotes.
But your behaviour is exemplary.
Your words have been, without exception, kind.
Do you have preconceived ideas of me?
If I am not yet typecast in your mind,
can I suggest the fool who will insist
on putting words in mouths she should have kissed?

Something Involving Us

I was so drunk, I don't remember much –
not how your body felt and not your arms
around me, not your dinner-suited touch
between two cars (not setting off alarms).
I do remember, though, the next day's drink,
your calmness, your I-still-respect-you smile,
and I remember that you said, 'I think
it's better if we leave it for a while.'
I next remember that you changed your mind,
and changed your mind, and changed your mind again,
as if, for you, something remained behind
(something I missed, not being sober then)
from that first night, something involving us,
that makes what's happened since seem worth the fuss.

DIMINISHING RETURNS

I will tell outright lies where you embellish.
Your yawn will be my cue to fall asleep.
Anyone who is watching us with relish
Will find that, where your talk and tricks are cheap,
Mine will be cast-offs. When you stop at kissing
I'll stop at shaking hands; you eye the clock,
I'll grab my watch and gasp at what I'm missing
And any door you close, I'll double-lock.
Operate slowly – I'll stand still forever.
Leave quickly – I will be the speed of light
Passing you on the way, and if we never
Do anything constructive, that's all right
(Though it will be a wasted chance) because
While casual observers say of you
'He led her on', of me they'll say, 'She was
The less enthusiastic of the two.'

This Calculating Field

A threatened field knows that it must give way
to a new road, starts to prepare for change,
turns, in anticipation, almost grey.
Everyone says *doesn't the grass look strange?*

The green that once inspired them to protest
has lost its charm, character, former fame.
Change can now safely be compared to rest.
The grass turns grey, ready to take the blame

as well as all effects of the assault.
Forget the luxury of looking good;
assume control. *Yes it is all my fault.*
If I did not turn bad, somebody would.

Can I have won and at the same time lost
all of my qualities that once appealed?
The outcome of a benefit and cost
equation is this calculating field

turning to grey. Your sadness in defending
becomes exhilaration in attack.
I can imagine only one good ending:
where you are glad that I will not be back.

LEAVING AND LEAVING YOU

When I leave your postcode and your commuting station,
When I leave undone the things that we planned to do
You may feel you have been left by association
But there is leaving and there is leaving you.

When I leave your town and the club that you belong to,
When I leave without much warning or much regret
Remember, there's doing wrong and there's doing wrong to
You, which I'll never do and I haven't yet,

And when I have gone, remember that in weighing
Everything up, from love to a cheaper rent,
You were all the reasons I thought of staying
And you were none of the reasons why I went

And although I leave your sight and I leave your setting
And our separation is soon to be a fact,
Though you stand beside what I'm leaving and forgetting,
I'm not leaving you, not if motive makes the act.

SHE HAS ESTABLISHED TITLE

She keeps the lies and popular support.
I take the condemnation and the truth.
I claim the chase; she has already caught.
Her permanence is balanced by my youth.
The afternoons are mine. She hogs the nights,
The public sphere encompassed by her rings.
She has established title. All the rights
Are hers. How fairly we divide these things.
Each of us has a quite substantial list
Of goodies, and I wouldn't choose to swap,
Like football cards, the knowledge I exist
For both the mortgage and the weekly shop,
My inventory for hers, if someone were
To ask, or wonder, what I might prefer.

YOUR DARLINGS

You call some women Darling and they fall
predictably in love, but say the same
to others (brighter ones, perhaps) and all
it means, they say, is that you're scared you'll call
one woman by another woman's name.

I know you get around a bit (I ought
to know) but can't presume to guess your fears
or what proportion of your conquests thought
your Darlings were sincere, or if the sort
of woman who believes her hopes and ears

predominates over the doubting kind
in your portfolio, whether a lapse
in disbelief makes a believing mind,
the lucky owner waking up to find
her prospects changed (to brighter ones, perhaps).

Some hunt and hunt until they find a fake
behind what either was or sounded true.
Those who are anything like me will take
the best interpretation, maybe make
fools of themselves, but make the most of you.

THE BRIDGING LINE

If, as it now appears,
a second time can lean across the ditch,
retrieve, like a dropped stitch,
the first, long in arrears,
how badly I've misjudged the last five years;

potholes beside our past
I thought they were, when all the time they've been
linear, in between,
travelling (if not fast)
towards next time, back from next time to last.

Tonight's no precipice,
merely one station on the bridging line
where incidents combine,
kiss throws a rope to kiss,
last time connects to next, next time to this –

a better fairytale
than scattered breadcrumbs on the forest floor;
wind howls, rain starts to pour
and soon you've lost your trail.
The bridging line is like a polished rail

beneath our years of space
that I can almost rest my hand upon.
I clutch it now you're gone,
find it reflects your face,
find I believe the next five years will race

straightforwardly ahead
as five have raced straightforwardly behind.
The gaps are redefined.
I hold my breath and tread
the bridging line towards a waiting bed.

Once When the Wind Blew

Our purses and our fumes
distinguish us, the normals, drys and oilies
who scan the tablecloths in auction rooms,
churn up the paper doilies

to find a cleaner head,
phrenology's bald, ornamental scalps,
black virtues sprinkled and black vices spread
on curves as white as Alps.

If we abandoned hair,
if, in its place, we could contrive to grow
lists of our qualities, complete but fair,
best and worst points on show,

the pain that it would save,
the moves from double into separate beds.
Imagine they are coming to engrave,
tomorrow, all our heads

and now's the time to dump
all that we judge unfit for public view.
We're talking ink (an enigmatic bump
is always subject to

interpretation, doubt,
with how it feels depending on the hand).
I would far rather have it all spelled out,
easy to understand.

Would I have felt that twinge
of sadness if I'd seen the word *inert*,
once when the wind blew, underneath your fringe,
or been so badly hurt

if just above your ear
capacity to cause unhappiness...
I could extend this game and this idea
but heads do not confess

failings to clumps of hair,
nor leave them stranded when the hair is gone,
but I know yours and when we meet somewhere
I'm going to carve them on.

HARDLY DEAR

I wouldn't buy you from a car boot sale,
not if your mind had been reduced to clear,
though you were overpriced at half a year.
With your significance cut down to scale

I could afford you. If you soon turned stale
I could point out that you were hardly dear
and that I'd had my money's worth, or near.
I wouldn't buy you from a car boot sale,

you or a size five shoe or books in braille –
I have no use for them. Let the sincere
stall-holder smile and say *a snip, a mere
pittance* as though he flogged the holy grail,

the greatest bargain in this hemisphere
rather than just a load of useless gear.
He might succeed with some. With me he'd fail.
I wouldn't buy you from a car boot sale.

TRIBUTE

For the first time I find it quite unnerving
That people's names are handed on to things.
No bench, so far, has proved itself deserving
Enough to bear your name. No hospice wings
Or students' union buildings will inherit,
If it has anything to do with me,
A name no other man could even merit
Let alone any slice of brick or tree.
I could be Lord Mayor with a town to listen
To my new street names; you would still be gone.
Now, as myself, with power to rechristen
No roads, there's still a tribute going on:
Though I call nothing by your name, I do
Practically nothing but call after you.

STEVEN'S SIDE

I am supporting Steven
as if I were a beam
    under his ceiling, even
though he is not a team.
    Under his ceiling even
a nightmare is a dream.

Steven and I have entered.
Some people have implied
    I would be too self-centred
to cheer for Steven's side,
    I would be too self-centred
to fail if Steven tried.

I am supporting Steven
as if I were a rail
    behind his curtain, even
though he is bound to fail.
    Behind his curtain even
a white net is a veil.

Steven is no performer.
He has no gift for sport.
　　I make no cool crowd warmer
by staging my support.
　　I make no cool crowd warmer,
adorn no tennis court

but I am supporting Steven
as if I were a pin
　　above his hemline, even
though he will never win.
　　Above his hemline even
a jacket is a skin.

I am supporting Steven.
I am at Steven's feet.
　　I put him first and even
give him a thing to beat.
　　I put him first and even
then he will not compete.

In Wokingham on Boxing Day at The Edinburgh Woollen Mill

Two earnest customers compare
a ribbed and unribbed sleeve.
I wonder what I'm doing here
and think I ought to leave,
get in my car and drive away.
   I stand beside the till
   in Wokingham on Boxing Day
   at The Edinburgh Woollen Mill.

All of the other shops are closed.
Most people are in bed.
Somehow I know that I'm supposed
to find an A-Z.
Somehow I sense I must obey
   an unfamiliar will
   in Wokingham on Boxing Day
   at The Edinburgh Woollen Mill.

I parked in a disabled space
so either I'm a cheat
or a debilitating case
of searching for your street
has started to erode away
   my locomotive skill
   in Wokingham on Boxing Day
   at The Edinburgh Woollen Mill,

somewhere perhaps you've never been.
I doubt you're into wool.
Even if mohair's not your scene
the atmosphere is full
of your proximity. I sway
      and feel a little ill
        in Wokingham on Boxing Day
        at The Edinburgh Woollen Mill.

The sales assistants wish me luck
and say they hope I find
the place I want. I have been stuck
with what I left behind,
with what I've been too scared to say,
      too scared to say until
        in Wokingham on Boxing Day
        at The Edinburgh Woollen Mill

I tell myself the time is now;
willingly I confess
my love for you to some poor cow
in an angora dress
whose *get lost loony* eyes convey
      her interest, which is nil,
        in Wokingham on Boxing Day
        at The Edinburgh Woollen Mill.

I find your house. You're still in bed.
I leave my gift and flee,
pleased with myself, not having said
how you can contact me,
driven by fears I can't allay,
   dreams I did not fulfil
   in Wokingham on Boxing Day
   at The Edinburgh Woollen Mill.

Chains are the most distressing shops.
They crop up everywhere.
The point at which the likeness stops
squeezes my lungs of air.
When I see jumpers on display
   I wish that I was still
   in Wokingham on Boxing Day
   at The Edinburgh Woollen Mill.

THREE LIGHT SIGN

There is a certain railway line
that runs straight through your town.
The level crossing's three light sign,
a therefore upside down,

has never blocked my route to you.
Perhaps my speed alarms
its sense of pace. When I drive through
the crossing's up in arms

but it has never told me stop
so I have never learned.
Attempts at sense have been a flop,
a therefore overturned.

You're always either in your room
or wandering about
outside. The crossing, I assume,
knows not to let you out.

I like to think it's in control
in case I go too far.
How underrated, on the whole,
most level crossings are.

You've given me a few bad nights —
ranting, withdrawn or worse
but when I see the crossing lights,
a therefore in reverse,

I know you don't mean any harm.
That's just the way it goes.
You, like the level crossing arm,
must have your highs and lows.

Sometimes two things that shouldn't mix
cannot be kept apart.
There is a rift too deep to fix
between a stop, a start,

a car, a train. But I see ways
over contested land,
watching the level crossing raise
its firm, permissive hand.

DRIVING ME AWAY

I caught the train to Waterloo,
The tube to Leicester Square.
Both did what they set out to do,
But neither could compare
With your closed eyes, your bitten nails
And the oddness you display.
You beat whatever's on the rails
At driving me away.

The coach to Gatwick last July
Did it in record time.
The plane, once it had deigned to fly,
Managed an upward climb.
You beat whatever's in the air
Or on the motorway
And do not even charge a fare
For driving me away.

The transit van I hired to move
For which I had to pack
Box after box, as if to prove
I wasn't coming back
And before driving which I paid
A visit to the tip,
Just to ensure the point was made:
This was a one way trip —

You beat that too. I could name loads
Of engine-powered things
In oceans, in the clouds, on roads,
With carriages or wings
But you could nudge them all off track
With the mad things you say.
No car could ever have your knack
Of driving me away.

There's not a lot that you can do
Well, or indeed at all.
I must appreciate your few
Talents. When taxis stall
Or when friends offer me a lift
And there's a slight delay
I am reminded of your gift
For driving me away.

Paint a Closed Window

We stood side by side.
Only George walked on.
You spoke and I replied
        but I had gone.

My gone did not depend
on anything you'd planned
and I did not extend
        even a hand.

My gone was not the sort
that might come back one day.
It was less felt than thought
        but most away.

I looked the same to you,
the arches and the cars,
and you could not see through
        my skin to bars.

My arrow pointed north.
Your word had lost its pass,
so no more back and forth
        from the hourglass.

My face became a chart
where pleasantries were drawn.
The binman pulled his cart
        around the lawn

where we stood once removed,
where we stand twice returned.
Nothing can be improved
        my gone has learned.

Foolish to have supposed
there might be other ways.
Paint a closed window, closed
        is how it stays.

I am prepared to face
how fleeting I have been
to you and to this place,
        that tree, the green

circle of grass, the stone.
From your first fixed-term kiss
I knew I could not own
        any of this.

MEN TO BURN

The same man every year;
though we have men to burn
we have sealed off that idea.
It is still one man's turn.

Every year one man glows,
his bright flesh chars to dim
and every next year shows
we are not rid of him.

He is propped against a fence.
His embroidered teeth still flash.
I part with twenty pence
to convert him into ash

but he won't stay ash for long.
He reappears in rags,
features not quite so strong
and his legs in dustbin bags.

He will keep coming back
for as long as he is allowed.
He will turn from gold to black
if he knows he's got a crowd.

I should have said this before
but I'm not prepared to pay
to bring him back once more
or to make him go away.

I don't like his grey sock face
or this year's cushion knees.
A good man in the first place
makes for better effigies.